MVFOL

Main Street Animal Shelter

Graphing

Suzanne Barchers

Publishing Credits

Dona Herweck Rice, *Editor-in-Chief*; Lee Aucoin, *Creative Director*; Don Tran, *Print Production Manager*; Sara Johnson, *Senior Editor*; Jamey Acosta, *Assistant Editor*; Neri Garcia, *Interior Layout Designer*; Stephanie Reid, *Photo Editor*; Rachelle Cracchiolo, M.A.Ed., *Publisher*

Image Credits

cover Perrush/Shutterstock; p.1 Perrush/Shutterstock; p.4 Getty Images/Thinkstock; p.5 (top left) Kuricheva Ekaterina/Shutterstock, (top right) Sharon Meredith/Shutterstock, (bottom left) Charlene Bayerle/Shutterstock, (bottom right) Monkey Business Images/Shutterstock; p.6 Epromocja/Shutterstock; p.8 Nebojsa S./Shutterstock; p.9 (top) Emin Ozkan/Shutterstock, (bottom left) Melinda Fawver/Shutterstock, (bottom right) Mark Herreid/Shutterstock; p.10 Jean Frooms/Shutterstock; p.12 Mark Poprocki/Dmitry Kosterev/Shutterstock; p.14 Forestpath/Shutterstock; p.16 Apollofoto/Shutterstock; p.18 SJLocke/iStockphoto; p.19 Franie/Flickr; p.20 (left) Feng Yu/Shutterstock, (right) Yuriy Korchagin/Shutterstock; p.22 Jule Berlin/Shutterstock; p.23 Matthew/Shutterstock; p.25 (top) Melinda Fawver/Shutterstock, (middle) Cveltri/iStockphoto, (bottom) Claudia Hung/iStockphoto; p.26 Spauln/Shutterstock; p.27 (left) Micimakin/Shutterstock, (right) Sonya Etchison/Shutterstock

Teacher Created Materials

5301 Oceanus Drive
Huntington Beach, CA 92649-1030
http://www.tcmpub.com

ISBN 978-1-4333-0429-3

©2011 Teacher Created Materials, Inc.
Reprinted 2012

Table of Contents

The Animal Shelter

There is a lot to do at Main Street Animal **Shelter**. It holds 80 animals. Dogs have to be walked. Cats need to be brushed.

Rabbits need to be cuddled.
Hamsters need their cages cleaned.
They all need to be fed!

The shelter may have dogs or cats that get lost. Sometimes people have to give up a pet. Those pets need new homes.

The shelter has cages for each kind of pet. The cages are almost full.

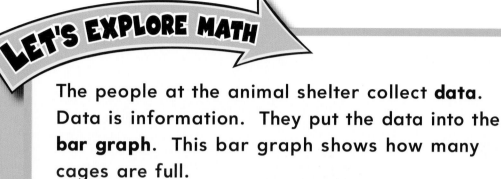

LET'S EXPLORE MATH

The people at the animal shelter collect **data**. Data is information. They put the data into the **bar graph**. This bar graph shows how many cages are full.

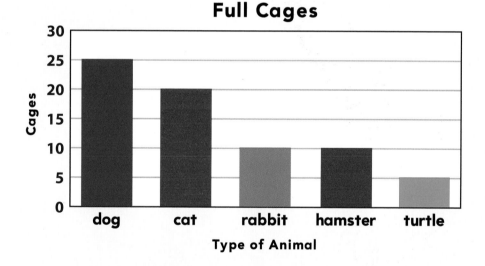

Full Cages

a. How many dog cages are full?

b. How many cat cages are full?

c. How many more dog cages than rabbit cages are full?

The Animals

The shelter has room for 30 dogs. Each dog needs the right-sized cage. A little dog can fit in a big cage. But a big dog can not fit in a little cage!

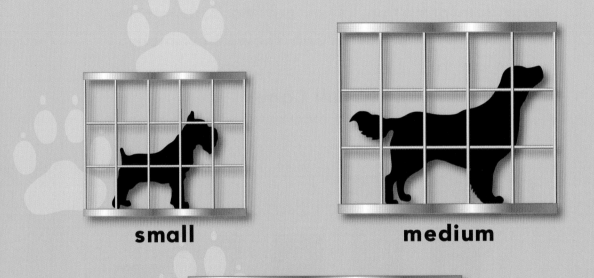

small   **medium**

big

Each dog gets a food dish, a chew toy, and a bed.

Each dog needs plenty of exercise.
Some dogs can play with the other dogs.
But some dogs need to be walked alone.

The workers make sure each dog has time outside. The dogs love playtime!

This **pictograph** shows how many dogs get walked in the morning, the afternoon, and the evening.

Time of Day Dogs are Walked

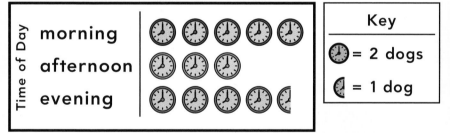

a. How many dogs are walked in the evening?

b. How many dogs are walked in the afternoon?

c. How many more dogs are walked in the morning than in the afternoon?

11

Cats at the shelter do not need to be walked. But they do need clean litter boxes.

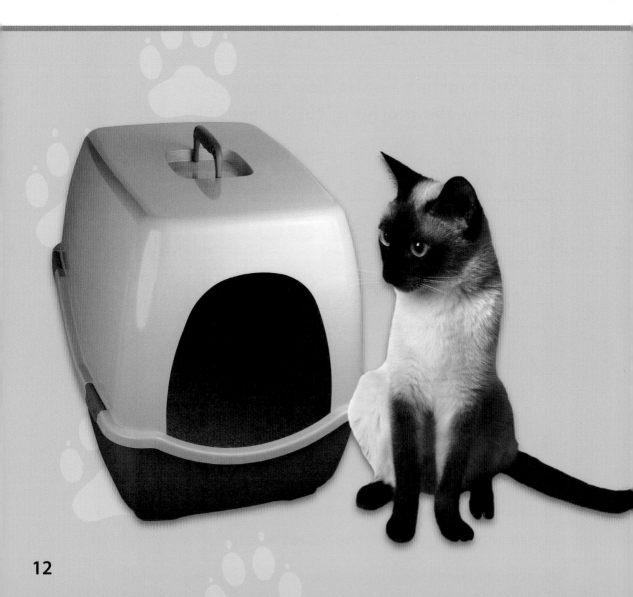

The boxes are cleaned 2 times each day. Clean boxes help keep the cages smelling fresh.

The **chart** below shows how much cat litter is used each day. In 1 day, 5 cats use 3 pounds of litter.

Pounds of Litter Used Daily

Number of Cats	Litter Used
5	3 pounds
10	5 pounds
15	8 pounds
20	10 pounds
25	13 pounds

a. If there are 10 cats at the shelter, how much litter is used in 1 day?

b. If there are 20 cats at the shelter, how much litter is used in 1 day?

You must love cats to work at a shelter. Cats need lots of cuddling. They need their coats brushed every day or two.

The cats purr when they are brushed. Cats purr when they are happy. Happy cats might get **adopted** sooner.

Cat Brushing Schedule		
Day of Week	9:00 A.M.	1:00 P.M.
Sunday	no brushing	no brushing
Monday	long-haired cats	short-haired cats
Tuesday	long-haired cats	
Wednesday	long-haired cats	short-haired cats
Thursday	long-haired cats	
Friday	long-haired cats	short-haired cats
Saturday	long-haired cats	

Rabbits have some of the same needs as cats. They love to be petted. Rabbits with long hair need to be brushed, too.

Rabbits need cages with room to hop and stretch. They need lots of fresh food and water.

This bar graph shows the number of rabbits and cats at the shelter.

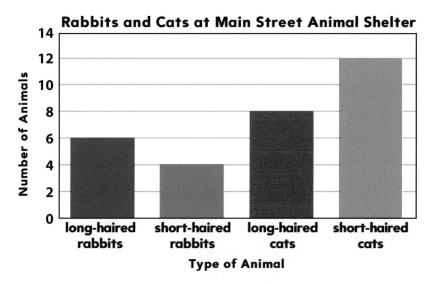

Rabbits and Cats at Main Street Animal Shelter

a. How many long-haired rabbits are at the shelter?

b. How many short-haired cats are at the shelter?

c. How many rabbits are there altogether?

A special doctor called a **veterinarian** checks the rabbits. The veterinarian makes sure that the rabbits are healthy.

Rabbits love to chew. They need good food and toys to chew on. Chewing keeps their teeth healthy.

Hamsters sleep during the day. They play at night. They like to dig. They like to make nests.

They run in their exercise wheels while the dogs and cats sleep. The workers keep the hamster cages in a quiet place.

Hamster Feeding Schedule	
Sunday	hamster mix
Monday	hamster mix and carrots
Tuesday	hamster mix
Wednesday	hamster mix and apple slices
Thursday	hamster mix
Friday	hamster mix, nuts, and seeds
Saturday	hamster mix

The turtles are quiet. They live in tanks. They have a place to stay warm and dry.

They also have water for swimming.

Volunteers

Shelters like to have **volunteers** help out. Volunteers may clean the cages. They may play with the dogs. They may pet the cats.

LET'S EXPLORE MATH

This bar graph shows the number of volunteers at the Main Street Animal Shelter. It also shows the jobs that the volunteers do.

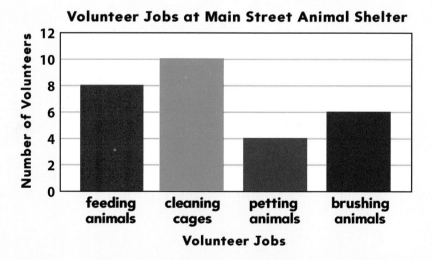

Volunteer Jobs at Main Street Animal Shelter

a. How many volunteers brush the animals?

b. What job has the least volunteers?

c. How many more volunteers feed the animals than brush the animals?

Some people make blankets for the dogs and cats. They may **donate** toys or food. These items are like gifts.

The shelter uses a pictograph to keep track of the items. They are happy when items are donated.

Items Donated to Main Street Animal Shelter

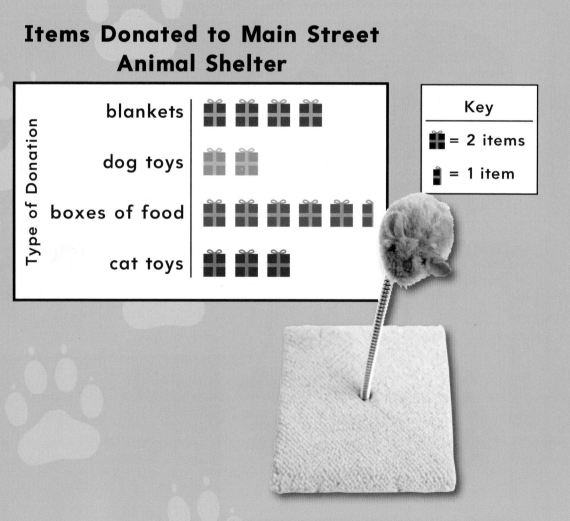

The best day is adoption day.
That is the day people come and
give the pets a new home!

Favorite Pets

Mr. Lee's class is gathering data about everyone's favorite pets. Each person in the class votes for his or her favorite pet. The votes are shown in the tally chart below. Make a bar graph using this data. Then answer the questions below.

Favorite Pets	
dog	卌 ‖
cat	卌 ‖‖
bird	卌 ‖
hamster	‖‖‖
turtle	‖

a. Which pet is liked most?

b. Which pet is liked least?

c. How many more people like birds than turtles?

Solve It!

Use the steps below to help you solve the problem.

Step 1: Copy this bar graph.

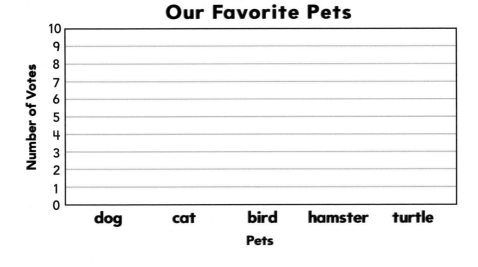

Step 2: Look at the tally chart. How many people like cats? Make a bar that shows that number of people.

Step 3: Look at the tally chart. How many people like dogs? Make a bar that shows that number of people.

Step 4: Finish the bar graph for the other animals. Then answer the questions.

Glossary

adopted—taken into a family

bar graph—a graph that uses bars to show information

chart—information that is put in columns and rows so that it is easy to read

data—a collection of information

donate—to give away something for free

pictograph—a graph that uses pictures and symbols to show information

shelter—a place where animals without homes are cared for

veterinarian—a doctor who takes care of animals

volunteers—people who work without pay

Index

Let's Explore Math

Page 7:
a. 25 dog cages
b. 20 cat cages
c. 15 more cages

Page 11:
a. 9 dogs
b. 6 dogs
c. 4 dogs

Page 13:
a. 5 pounds
b. 10 pounds

Page 17:
a. 6 long-haired rabbits
b. 12 short-haired cats
c. 10 rabbits

Page 24:
a. 6 volunteers
b. petting animals
c. 2 more volunteers

Solve the Problem

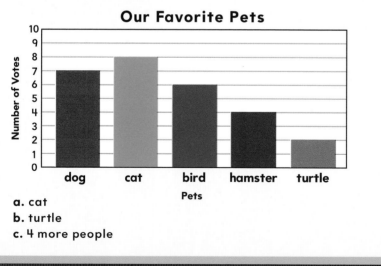

Our Favorite Pets

a. cat
b. turtle
c. 4 more people